GOD FINDS RELIGION

A Short Play
by
Royce Roeswood

Cast of Characters

2m, 1f, 2 flexible

GOD: For the purposes of this play, a male. Dressed a little sloppy today, T-shirt and jeans.

GABRIEL: God's right-hand angel. Female. Professional, put together, business suit. Little wings and a halo.

RAUL: God's friend. Male. Wears red.

MEGA-GOD: Long-flowing white robes. Cast as you wish.

ULTRA-GOD: A superior cybernetic organism.

Scene
Heaven. A coffee shop.

Time
Now.

God Finds Religion
© Royce Roeswood
Trade Edition, 2015
ISBN 978-1-63092-068-5

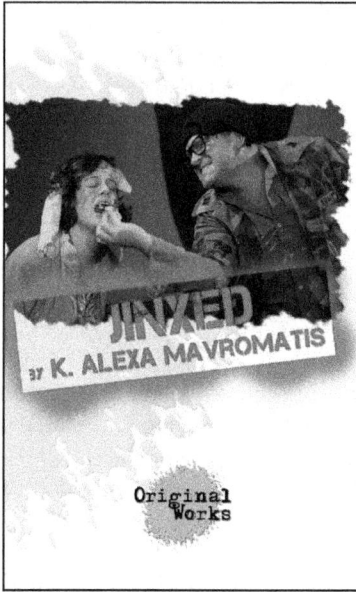

<u>Jinxed</u> by K. Alexa Mavromatis

Synopsis: The apocalypse has hit and no one was prepared. Only Stringbean and Meatloaf remain. With food and companionship in short supply these lone survivors engage in a post-apocalyptic fight over whoopie pies, playground games… and so much more.

Cast Size: 1 Male, 1 Female

"God Finds Religion" was produced at the Rocky Mountain Short Play Festival at Red Rocks Community College in Lakewood, CO, on November 6, 2014. The original cast and crew was as follows:

God: Leodis Smith
Gabriel: Kacie Couch
Raul: Tom Saleco
Mega-God: Jason Ponder
Ultra-God: Jeff Munger

Director: James O'Leary
Lighting Designer: Gail Gober
Sound Designer: Steve Stevens
Set Designer: Pamela Jamruszka Mencher
Costume Designer: Caroline Smith

GOD FINDS RELIGION

(AT RISE: GOD and GABRIEL are sitting at a table.)

GABRIEL: *(reading from her things)* Prayers down seventeen million, faith up point eight million, church attendance down three point five million, guilt up six million, and fear up twelve million to an all-time high of three hundred and seventy six billion.

(She pauses. GOD is staring off into space, idly fingering his coffee cup.)

GABRIEL: God. God! Earth to God!

GOD: Hmm?

GABRIEL: Did you catch any of that?

GOD: Yeah, yeah, stuff up and down, all time high, numbers numbers numbers.

GABRIEL: Okay, just making sure you're still there.

GOD: Don't worry, Gabriel, I'm here. Just waiting for the caffeine to kick in.

GABRIEL: I've got this morning's prayers if you're ready.

GOD: Might as well get started.

(GABRIEL pulls out a massive folder, reads through these relatively quickly)

GABRIEL: Okay, first one. Maria Alvarez of Sao Paulo is asking for your blessing over her tomato plants.

GOD: *(with a careless wave of the hand)* Bless.

GABRIEL: Little Alexander Petrovich of Oslo is praying for world peace again.

GOD: *(as before)* Bless.

GABRIEL: Charles West of Johannesburg, South Africa, wants your blessing for this afternoon's history test.

GOD: Did he study?

GABRIEL: *(looks at the paper)* Uh ... yes.

GOD: Bless.

GABRIEL: Kim Tashamoto of Tokyo his having pains in her ankle again.

GOD: Tell her go to the doctor already.

GABRIEL: *(prodding)* God.

GOD: Bless.

GABRIEL: Chelsea Hansard of San Antonio wants a drum set for Christmas.

GOD: Why is she asking me? She should ask her parents.

GABRIEL: Please, let's just get these done.

GOD: *(sarcastic)* Has she been naughty or nice?

GABRIEL: She goes to church ever week, prays daily, tries her best to tell the truth, took that candy bar she stole back to the store and asked for forgiveness.

GOD: *(victorious)* No drum set for Chelsea Hansard!

GABRIEL: Why? She's a very good Christian.

GOD: I work in mysterious ways.

GABRIEL: Alright, you're the boss. Next one. Four thousand, five hundred and twenty-six fans want you to help the Diamondbacks win this Tuesday's game.

GOD: How many for the Rockies?

GABRIEL: Uh ... five thousand thirty-one.

GOD: Rockies have it. That's good, I have money on them.

GABRIEL: Jenna Marshall of Tampa Bay wants you to safely bring her husband back from his tour of duty.

GOD: Not my call.

GABRIEL: God, please, you're being impossible today.

GOD: I had nothing to do with it. People decide when to start wars, so people have to decide when to end them. It's not my responsibility, goddammit.

GABRIEL: Please don't take the Lord's name in vain.

GOD: It's my name, me-dammit.

GABRIEL: You really should try to set a good example.

GOD: Fine.

GABRIEL: Are you feeling okay today? You seem really out of it.

GOD: No, it's nothing, really. I'm just tired.

GABRIEL: Okay.

GOD: How many prayers left?

GABRIEL: *(motioning towards the giant folder)* We barely even started.

(GOD crumples with a large sigh)

GABRIEL: We could do them tomorrow, if you really want.

GOD: *(after a pause)* Yeah, why don't we?

GABRIEL: That's a lot of people's prayers that are going unanswered, but ...

GOD: Eh, what else is new?

(beat)

GABRIEL: Are you sure you're feeling okay?

GOD: Yeah, why?

GABRIEL: You're not yourself today.

GOD: I've ... had a lot on my mind.

GABRIEL: *(becoming less business-like, more personable)* Like what?

GOD: No, it's dumb.

GABRIEL: You can talk to me. How come we never talk anymore?

GOD: You know how busy we've been.

GABRIEL: We're relaxing now. It is Sunday, after all.

GOD: Gotta rest sometime.

GABRIEL: So ... talk to me.

GOD: About what?

GABRIEL: Anything. Life.

GOD: Life. Right. That's a pretty small subject.

GABRIEL: Right.

(They share a small laugh)

GOD: I don't know, it just wears you down sometimes, you know? The day-to-day grind.

GABRIEL: Yeah.

GOD: It makes you wonder ...

GABRIEL: What?

GOD: *(shrug)* You know.

GABRIEL: *(she honestly has no idea)* No, I don't.

GOD: It's like ... what is this all for? Why are we here? Stuff like that.

GABRIEL: I don't wonder about stuff like that.

GOD: You don't?

GABRIEL: No. I know why I'm here. God has a purpose for everyone, and my purpose is to be your right-hand angel. So I work as hard as I can to fulfill my purpose, which is God's purpose. Your purpose.

GOD: I have a purpose for everyone?

GABRIEL: Yep.

GOD: Guess I dropped the ball on that one.

GABRIEL: Pardon?

GOD: Never mind. I don't know if I'm doing what I want to with my life.

GABRIEL: What do you mean? Of course you are.

GOD: I don't feel like I'm doing anything.

GABRIEL: Of course you do! You help people.

GOD: Do I?

GABRIEL: Yes! Why so many questions?

GOD: It's like, people can't see me. They can't hear me. I can't really effect anything.

GABRIEL: Miracles. You do miracles.

GOD: What was the last miracle I did? Hmm?

(GABRIEL is stuck)

GOD: That's what I thought.

GABRIEL: But you did a whole bunch a long time ago.

(GOD gives her a glance, 'are you for real?')

GABRIEL: What?

GOD: C'mon. People see good stuff in the world and assume I had something to do with it, when really it happens the same way that the bad stuff does. And when they can't explain stuff they just put it on me. Thanks, people, but I really don't deserve that much credit.

GABRIEL: I think you just need a good night's rest and everything will feel better in the morning.

GOD: I would, but I told Raul I'd meet him here and he'll be here any minute.

GABRIEL: Raul? Who's Raul?

GOD: A friend.

GABRIEL: Okay.

GOD: What? Am I not allowed to have friends?

GABRIEL: I didn't say that.

GOD: But you thought it.

GABRIEL: I didn't! Why are you attacking me?

GOD: Am I not allowed to have friends?

GABRIEL: Yes! Of course you are! Friends are great! I love friends!

GOD: Okay!

GABRIEL: Okay!

(A long pause)

GOD: God, I am snippy today. I'm sorry.

GABRIEL: It's okay.

GOD: I'm sorry.

GABRIEL: We all have bad days.

GOD: Deep breath.

(He takes a deep breath)

GOD: There.

GABRIEL: There.

GOD: Okay, but there's still one more question I have.

GABRIEL: What?

(But before he can ask, RAUL enters.)

RAUL: Hey!

GOD: Raul! Speak of the devil, we were just talking about you.

RAUL: Only good things, I hope.

(RAUL goes over and puts his arm around GOD. GABRIEL watches this very carefully.)

GOD: Raul, this is my assistant, Gabriel.

RAUL: I'm so excited to finally meet you.

GABRIEL: *(stiffly putting out her hand to shake)* Charmed.

GOD: Sit down.

(They make room for him)

RAUL: I hope I'm not interrupting any important God stuff.

GOD: No, no. Gabriel and I were just having a little philosophical chat.

RAUL: Fun! *(to Gabriel:)* You know, God is so smart. I could talk to him forever. It's like he knows everything.

GOD: Stop it.

RAUL: Don't be modest. Last night, in the hot tub, we were talking about --

(GOD clears his throat, shakes his head)

RAUL: Oh. *(at GABRIEL, knowingly)* Oh, I see.

(There is an awkward silence.)

GABRIEL: So, Raul, what do you do?

RAUL: Oh, I work down in Purgatory.

GOD: With the kids.

RAUL: The little kids who die before they can understand God's word. They're so sweet. Shame they can't come straight here.

GOD: *(in jest)* I don't make the rules.

(GOD and RAUL laugh.)

GABRIEL: Yes you do.

GOD: Yeah, I know, it was a joke.

GABRIEL: Oh.

RAUL: You know, God, I was meaning to ask you, you're infinitely good, right?

GOD: People seem to think to seem so, sure.

RAUL: Then why don't you just let everyone into heaven?

GOD: *(he's been through this before)* It's complicated.

GABRIEL: You have to give people incentive to live a good life.

GOD: Otherwise they mess everything up.

RAUL: Which they do anyway.

GOD: Which they do anyway, yes.

RAUL: But it's still not very fair. Some people never even hear about you.

GOD: Like?

RAUL: The kids I work with. Or the thousands of years of civilization in the Pre-Columbian Americas.

GOD: Yeah, well ...

RAUL: It's not really infinitely good to judge people when they're not even given a chance. You could at least show yourself to give people a chance.

GOD: I can't.

RAUL: Why not?

GOD: They all have free will.

RAUL: But you're all-knowing. You know what they're going to do anyway.

GOD: Yeah, I guess.

RAUL: And it's not interfering with free will anyway. If you would present yourself to everyone, they still have a choice whether to accept or reject you. It's still a choice. But you don't do that.

GOD: I don't do that.

RAUL: Why not? You can. You're infinitely powerful. You can do anything.

GOD: Eh ... *(shrugs)* ... I work in mysterious ways.

RAUL: That's your answer?

GABRIEL: It's the best we've been able to come up with so far.

GOD: Sorry. I wish I knew, but I don't. It's kind of a stupid system.

RAUL: But I thought you were infinitely just.

GOD: Nope. Listen, I can't be infinitely good, infinitely powerful, all-knowing, and just all at the same time. I can only do so much.

RAUL: It's okay, honey. I'm sorry. *(he touches GOD'S hand)* I thought I'd ask.

GOD: It's alright. You're not the only one.

GABRIEL: *(to GOD)* Is there something you're not telling me?

GOD: About what?

GABRIEL: He's not just a *friend*, is he?

(A long pause)

GOD: Alright. I didn't know how to say this, because I was afraid of how you were going to react, but... Raul is my boyfriend.

GABRIEL: Why did you try to hide it from me? Why didn't you tell me up front?

GOD: Because I knew you would react like this.

RAUL: He is all knowing, after all.

GABRIEL: Do you think I'm *stupid*?

GOD: No!

GABRIEL: I can't believe this. We take one day, *one day* off, and everything goes to hell. Pardon the expression.

GOD: No offense taken.

GABRIEL: But, you – I can't believe – it's in your book!

GOD: Yeah, I know.

GABRIEL: You know?

GOD: Yeah...

GABRIEL: *(motioning to GOD and RAUL)* So what is this then?

GOD: Well, I was thinking the other day, and I realized, it's all love, right? And I'm down with love. It's what I'm all about, right? So, what's the big deal?

GABRIEL: But you wrote it in your book.

GOD: I've been meaning to write a new edition, but I'm never happy with the translations. And a good ghostwriter is so hard to find.

GABRIEL: So, what, you're just changing everything around on me, is that it? If I can't believe one part of your book, how can I believe the other parts?

GOD: You know, yesterday, I would have said to just believe. But today, I'm not so sure.

RAUL: What are you saying?

GOD: I'm saying ... I don't know if I exist.

GABRIEL: What? Of course you do. You're right there.

GOD: I know. But so much doesn't make sense. I have all these questions. I can't fit it all together.

GABRIEL: Have faith.

RAUL: Yeah.

GOD: No! I want to know! Faith is an excuse for ignorance.

GABRIEL: Okay. We can figure it out. What do you want to know?

GOD: Where did I come from?

GABRIEL: Easy.

RAUL: Is it?

GABRIEL: I know where I came from.

RAUL: You do.

GABRIEL: God made me.

GOD: I did?

GABRIEL: It's the only thing that makes sense. How could millions of years of evolution make something like the eye? The circulatory system?

RAUL: You're an archangel. You don't have a circulatory system.

GABRIEL: You're missing the point. We were designed. We had to have an intelligent designer. It's the only way.

GOD: That doesn't help me. So I designed you. What about me?

GABRIEL: Well, you're the intelligent designer. You're infinitely more intelligent then any of us. And you're infinitely powerful. Which means --

GOD: *(finally realizing)* I was created by something even more intelligent and powerful.

GABRIEL: I was going to say you created yourself.

GOD: No, no, you see? Everything's okay now.

GABRIEL: What could have possibly made you?

GOD: Mega-god.

RAUL: Mega-god?

GOD: *(absolutely enthralled and relieved)* Yes. And Mega-god loves me, and has a plan for me, and I don't have to worry about anything, because if I do good, when I get to Mega-heaven, everything will be explained.

GABRIEL: I don't know about that.

GOD: Why not? It works for you people. Why not for me?

RAUL: But you have no proof that Mega-god exists.

GOD: But if I pray hard enough and believe, Mega-god will be revealed. *(kneeling down and praying)* Mega-god, I know you're out there, and I believe in you, so if you could reveal yourself to me, I'll know everything is okay.

(Nothing happens.)

GABRIEL: God, please.

(Then, suddenly, MEGA-GOD bursts into the room, full of splendor)

MEGA-GOD: *(to GOD)* Come to me, my child.

GOD: Mega-god! I knew you'd come.

(GOD rushes into MEGA-GOD's loving arms.)

RAUL: Oh, this is so sweet.

GABRIEL: No, no, this can't be happening.

MEGA-GOD: Everything is going to be alright.

GABRIEL: Don't you realize what you've done? This starts an infinite regression. If you were created by something more intelligent and powerful than yourself, then that means whatever created you had to have a creator as well.

MEGA-GOD: Of course. Let me introduce you to my creator, Ultra-god.

(The powerful robot ULTRA-GOD explodes in with ten times the splendor)

ULTRA-GOD: I am Ultra-god two thousand, burning with the flame of a trillion fiery suns!

GABRIEL: No, no, there's no end to it, don't you see?

ULTRA-GOD: All confusion will be destroyed by my powerful and immaculate laser sword! THERE IS NO NEED TO FEAR!

GABRIEL: Oh my god!

GOD + MEGA-GOD + ULTRA-GOD: Yes?

GABRIEL: Ahhhh!!!

(GABRIEL rushes off the stage in a fit of logical discrepancies.)

GOD: Wait, Gabriel, everything is going to be okay!

(GOD rushes after her.)

RAUL: God, wait for me!

(RAUL follows. Only MEGA-GOD and ULTRA-GOD remain. Awkward pause.)

MEGA-GOD: So.

ULTRA-GOD: So.

MEGA-GOD: He left his coffee.

ULTRA-GOD: Is it still hot?

MEGA-GOD: *(checks)* Nope.

ULTRA-GOD: All coffee must be hot! Thus decrees Ultra-god two thousand!

(ULTRA-GOD destroys the coffee with the laser sword. Another awkward pause.)

MEGA-GOD: Are you feeling okay?

ULTRA-GOD: Why?

MEGA-GOD: You seem ... upset.

ULTRA-GOD: I've ... been thinking about a lot of stuff lately.

MEGA-GOD: *(inviting ULTRA-GOD to sit)* Why don't you tell me all about it?

(END OF PLAY)

www.ingramcontent.com/pod-product-compliance
Lightning Source LLC
Chambersburg PA
CBHW060809040426
42331CB00046BB/2442